Original title:
Ripe for Love

Copyright © 2025 Creative Arts Management OÜ
All rights reserved.

Author: Isaac Ravenscroft
ISBN HARDBACK: 978-1-80586-416-5
ISBN PAPERBACK: 978-1-80586-888-0

Seasons' Embrace

In springtime's glow, we danced around,
With tulips giggling on the ground.
Summer's heat brought sun-kissed bliss,
Ice cream drips and a silly kiss.

Autumn leaves in colors bright,
We jumped in piles, oh what a sight!
Winter's chill, a cozy spree,
Hot cocoa shared, just you and me.

Blossoming Promises

A daisy's wink, a rose's grin,
We whispered secrets, oh what a win!
Sunflowers swayed with a playful tease,
Turns out love grows with the bees.

Tulips twirled in a breezy dance,
Pollen allergies? Just take a chance!
Petals tossed in a flowery fight,
We skated home under moonlight.

Tangy Adventures

Lemons rolling down the street,
Chasing oranges, what a treat!
Strawberries giggled, sweet and red,
Wherever we wander, love's ahead.

A pineapple wore a funny hat,
We both laughed, oh imagine that!
Juicy moments, sticky and bright,
In this fruit salad, love takes flight.

Fields of Heartbeats

In fields of daisies, hearts collide,
With butterflies as our goofy guide.
We chased rainbows and painted skies,
Giggles floated like fireflies.

The grass tickled as we rolled and spun,
Life's a game that's always fun.
With every laugh, and every cheer,
Our quirky love grows year by year.

Sipping from the Chalice of Connection

In twilight's glow, we share a drink,
With comic tales, and laughter's wink.
A teacup full of sweet devotion,
Spilled over, like a wild ocean.

We toast to dreams, both big and small,
An awkward dance, we stumble, fall.
Yet with each giggle, sparks ignite,
In quirks and quips, we find delight.

When Stars Align in Harmony.

On a goofy night, the stars conspire,
With pizza slices, we fuel our fire.
Laughing loud at cosmic plans,
While joking 'bout our alien clans.

We twirl beneath this vast expanse,
In mismatched socks, we take our chance.
When fate's a dice, we roll with glee,
Each quirk pulls us closer, can't you see?

Fruits of Affection

A fruit bowl filled with lots of fun,
A banana slip on which to run.
Mango smiles, with giggles to share,
Peachy moments float in the air.

With grape expectations, we pursue,
Kiwis bounce, like thoughts anew.
In silly talks, our hearts will blend,
In this sweet orchard, we transcend.

Harvesting Hearts

With baskets full, we roam the patch,
Plucking dreams, a whimsical match.
Pumpkin giggles, cornfield spins,
Silly traits, like harvest wins.

Under the sun, we chase the breeze,
Skipping past, like playful bees.
In this field of blushing fun,
Together we shine, two hearts as one.

Ripples of Romance

In a pond of silly charms,
Two frogs dance on soft alarms,
They croak and hop, a jolly tune,
Underneath the sassy moon.

With a splash, they sway and glide,
Caught in a wobbly love ride,
Lily pads make a fine stage,
For their froggy, funny page.

The Essence of Us

You steal my fries, I grin wide,
In ketchup puddles, we confide,
With goofy laughs and silly jibes,
Together we create fun vibes.

Whispers sweet, in snorts we share,
Pasta stuck in your wild hair,
Every meal's a merry jest,
In our clumsy love, we're blessed.

Enchanted by the Seasons

Winter coats and snowball fights,
Your snowman gives me silly frights,
Giggling 'neath a sky so gray,
Who knew frost could lead to play?

Spring brings blooms of wobbly cars,
We race our bikes beneath the stars,
Dandelions in your hair,
A crown of fluff, with love to spare.

Blooming Hearts in Full Color

In gardens where the daisies poke,
You paint my world with every joke,
With rainbows made from silly strings,
Our laughter flies on fluttering wings.

Through petals bright, our hearts embark,
With a potted plant, we leave a mark,
A cactus hug might sting a bit,
But love blooms on in bits that fit.

Juicy Secrets

In a fruit basket, you can find,
Secrets sweetly intertwined.
Lemons giggle, apples grin,
Whispering where love's begun.

Bananas dance in a funny way,
Telling tales of a bright buffet.
The berries blush, oh what a sight,
As laughter echoes through the night.

Echoes of Euphoria

In the orchard where jokes collide,
Peaches blush from the laughter inside.
Pineapples sing, their crowns held high,
While cherries chuckle, oh me, oh my!

Grapes roll around, they can't keep still,
With joy on the vine, they never chill.
Tickled by breezes and sunlit ways,
They gossip sweetly about their days.

The Flavor of Togetherness

Strawberries pinch and giggle tight,
Wishing the blueberries could join the flight.
With each bouncy step, flavors collide,
Creating a bond in fruity pride.

Kiwis waltz with zest and flair,
While tangerines toss their hair everywhere.
In this garden of fun and cheer,
Together we savor, far and near.

Sunlit Promises

In sun-drenched fields where laughter grows,
Tomatoes wink and peek their nose.
Under the sun, it's a comical race,
To see who can spread joy with grace.

Cucumbers pose, striking a stance,
As carrots twirl in a weird dance.
Amidst the warmth, friendships beam,
In this garden, we live the dream.

In Currents of Desire

The fish swam by with a wink,
They whispered secrets, not a word of ink.
Tangled in nets of flirty glee,
Catching feelings, just wait and see.

With every splash, they danced around,
Under the waves, a smirk was found.
The seaweed swayed like a playful tease,
As crabs caroused with hilarious ease.

Under the Canopy of Trust

Beneath the leaves, two squirrels plotted,
Chasing their tails, both quite knotted.
A leap in the air, a whimsical dive,
Who said trusting friends can't arrive?

With acorns shared in the tune of delight,
They giggled in shadows, a comical sight.
Bumping and thumping, they played all day,
In their canopy world, playful and gay.

On the Edge of Desire

At the cliff's side, a goat did prance,
With wobbly legs, it took a chance.
A leap of faith over rocks so sheer,
In the crowd below, a laugh or a cheer!

With bleats of joy echoing wide,
The daring goat danced with silly pride.
Down below, the onlookers swayed,
As laughter ignited, the fear just frayed.

Picking Daisies and Desires

In fields of green, the daisies gleamed,
With each pluck, a silly scheme.
"Loves me, loves me not," they sang out loud,
While butterflies giggled, gathering a crowd.

Spinning in circles, they dropped more blooms,
The sun laughed bright, dispelling glooms.
Each petal tossed became a sign,
In this wacky garden, all would be fine.

When Passion Sparks

In the kitchen, you burned the toast,
But we laughed, and we did the most.
Flour on our faces, what a sight,
Cooking together late at night.

You dance like a chicken, it's quite the show,
I can't help but join in, go with the flow.
Your two left feet, they charm the crowd,
In this quirky moment, I'm feeling proud.

Garden of Yearning

In a garden where daisies bloom,
I watched you dig a giant hole with a broom.
You said it was for treasures galore,
But all you found was a rubber ducky in store.

Digging deeper, you hit a shoe,
Maybe a message from a shoe-loving zoo?
Yet every mishap makes me cheer,
In this odd garden, I want you near.

Sweet Serenades and Starlit Nights

Under the stars, you croon off-key,
I pretend it's smooth, but chuckle with glee.
A serenade intended for romance,
Turns into laughter, an awkward dance.

Your shadow leaps like a willy-nilly,
Too caught up in rhythms that get really silly.
Yet beneath the giggles and silly tunes,
My heart skips beats under the moon.

Cradled in Kindness

You made me hot cocoa that was a shade gray,
Improvising was definitely not your forte.
But when you smiled, all worries were gone,
In the fluff of marshmallows, love is drawn.

In a blanket fort made of pillows and dreams,
We giggle and whisper, sharing our schemes.
With your silly jokes, you lighten my heart,
In this cozy chaos, we'll never part.

Love's Rich Tapestry

In a garden so bright, with colors aglow,
A pair of old socks lie, one orange, one blue.
They start a dance, both twirling around,
Giggling at love that's caught by a shoe.

Butterflies chuckle, as they flit by,
At mismatched lovers who can't even try.
With hiccuping laughs and a splash of bright cheese,
They toast to the moments that tickle and tease.

Fragrant Memories

In the kitchen, a pot simmers soft and sweet,
Filled with spices that jiggle from head to feet.
The cat's doing ballet, while the dog's on the floor,
Both dreaming of dinner and maybe some more.

A spatula winks, as it flips by the stove,
Mixing up flavors, with a little of gove.
Each whiff of the soup brings back the fun,
Of when love was served on a lazy Sunday run.

Sweetened by Time

A jar of old jelly sits up on the shelf,
It laughs every day at its own sticky self.
With whispers of cherries and sugary dreams,
It jokes about love and all its sweet themes.

When spread on warm toast, it creates quite the scene,
Two bites and they're dancing, a sugary sheen.
With giggles and crumbs trailing down to the floor,
The kitchen's a circus, who could ask for more?

When Hearts Blossom

When flowers unfurl in a bright sunny park,
Two squirrels debate 'bout love in the dark.
With acorns for gifts and a flick of their tails,
They spin silly circles, telling tall tales.

The sun peeks through clouds, casting rays full of cheer,
As these furry romantics hold hands without fear.
With leaps and with bounds, they frolic around,
In a love that feels silly, yet truly profound.

Lush Landscapes of Affection

In fields of giggles, we shall play,
Chasing butterflies throughout the day,
With silly hats and snacks to share,
Our laughter echoes in the air.

A painted fence with colors bright,
We dance like fireflies in the night,
With corny jokes and winks that tease,
Our love grows like the tallest trees.

Embracing What's Primed

Two hearts that bounce like rubber balls,
In grocery aisles and shopping malls,
We trip on dreams, so sweet and grand,
And giggle softly, hand in hand.

We try to cook, but smoke arises,
Our pizza skills are full of surprises,
Yet through the chaos, love does bloom,
In this zany kitchen, there's still room.

The Sweet Taste of Togetherness

With cookie dough and frosting mess,
We bake a cake to share, no less,
Each batter splatter, a work of art,
Sweet moments that pull at the heart.

In this delight, we take a bite,
Love served warm, it feels so right,
A pinch of fun, a sprinkle of cheer,
Each spoonful whispers, 'Do come near!'

Gardens of Longing

In pots of whims, our plants will grow,
Each bloom a giggle, each leaf a show,
We water dreams with silly songs,
In this garden, nothing feels wrong.

Dancing daisies wave and cheer,
They whisper secrets, sweet and clear,
With every petal, a playful sigh,
We laugh together, you and I.

Blooms of the Heart

In a garden of giggles, hearts do sway,
With petals of laughter, come out to play.
The sun winks slyly, it knows our plot,
And bees take notes on the jokes we've got.

We chat with the daisies, share silly dreams,
While tulips join in with their whims and schemes.
Be careful with pruning—don't snip the fun,
Or the blooms might just fly off to chase the sun!

Enchanted Harvest

In fields of mischief, we plant our cheer,
With pumpkins that giggle, and corn that's clear.
A tomato winks as it ripens with grace,
Joking with cucumbers, what a fine place!

We gather the harvest, with jokes in our sack,
Eggplants are chuckling, come join the quack!
With every sweet nibble, our laughter expands,
Farming's an art, and fun's our command.

Raindrops of Affection

When raindrops fall, they dance on the ground,
Each splash a giggle, a playful sound.
Umbrellas wobble with each silly spin,
As puddles invite us, 'Come jump right in!'

A rainbow appears with a cheeky grin,
It knows how we laugh whenever we spin.
So let's splash together, let worries soak,
With each droplet's tickle, we share a joke!

Delicate Tendrils

Vines twist and twirl like dancers so spry,
Whispering secrets beneath the blue sky.
With delicate tendrils, they reach and entwine,
In a tangled embrace, they flourish and shine.

Each leaf tells a story, a humorous tale,
Of caterpillars munching, on fingers they sail.
So join in the fun, don't let it get lost,
In the garden of giggles, we'll laugh at the cost!

Bursting with Affection

In my garden, hearts do bloom,
Each petal whispers, 'Make some room!'
Squirrels gossip, and bees do dance,
As love bites back like a pair of pants.

The tulips giggle, can't hold it in,
They mock the roses, 'What's the win?'
Daffodils chuckle, 'We're quite the crew!'
While dandelions plot a love debut.

A Symphony of Petals

Blossoms jive in a floral band,
Their tunes are quirky, oh so grand!
The hummingbirds laugh, sipping sweet tea,
While butterflies fold their ribbons with glee.

Tulip trumpets blare with cheer,
'Gather around, for spring is near!'
But daisies trip, as they spin and twirl,
Saying, 'Catch us, if you can, you whirl!'

Overflowing with Joy

Bouncing like balls in a meadow wide,
Crickets play tunes, with joy as their guide.
Sunshine winks, and clouds giggle bright,
While frogs leap over with sheer delight.

The laughter echoes through fields of green,
Chasing shadows where we've all been.
A picnic's set, with pies that tease,
But ants arrive, 'We're here to seize!'

Cherished Moments Under the Sun

Sunbeams dance on our silly heads,
As we tell stories on grassy beds.
Giggles bubble like soda pop,
While sandwiches disappear non-stop.

The sun's a matchmaker, so we know,
Drifting along like boats in the flow.
With lemonade splashes, oh what a scene,
Summer memory, both fun and serene!

The Orchard of Dreams

In the orchard where apples giggle,
Oranges dance with a quirky wiggle,
Plums throw parties, all fruity and bright,
Bananas slip on laughter all night.

Cherries flirt with the breezy air,
Peaches blush, but they just don't care,
A pear named Larry tells bad jokes,
While grapefruits roll and all of them poke.

Underneath the boughs, love's in the air,
Kissing the fruits, cheeky pairs to share,
Grapes sing songs, keep the rhythm alive,
In this orchard, it's a zany jive.

So join the fun in this silly expanse,
Where every fruit gets a silly dance,
With laughter and cheer, what a tasty spree,
In the orchard of dreams, come laugh with me!

Blossoms in Twilight

In twilight's glow, flowers tease the moon,
Daffodils shuffle, getting in tune,
Tulips giggle in their chatty huddle,
While daisies play hide and seek in a muddle.

Petals whisper secrets, oh so sweet,
While vibrant hues compete for a seat,
Cacti wear crowns, looking quite droll,
Laughing with roses, taking a stroll.

Evening brings winks from fragrant blooms,
As stars spout jokes and take over the rooms,
The garden's alive, with chatter and cheer,
In this twilight dance, love's drawing near.

So come take a step in this whimsical place,
Where blossoms and laughter go hand in hand,
In a bouquet of giggles, we all intertwine,
In the twilight, we flourish, an unending line.

Savoring the Moment

On a picnic blanket, sandwiches sigh,
As ants sneak in, oh my, oh my!
Pickles joke with the bread on the side,
While lemonade winks, bubbling with pride.

A cookie starts dancing, oh what a sight,
Chips whistle tunes, feeling just right,
A pie throws a fit, it's a fruit-tastic show,
As flavors collide in a savory glow.

Gobbling up laughs with bites of delight,
Savoring moments, everything feels right,
With crumbs and giggles littering our space,
In this feast of joy, life's a soft embrace.

So grab a snack and jump in the fun,
With flavors and chuckles, we've only begun,
Let's savor each giggle, each tasty affair,
In this moment of joy, let's scatter our care.

Tender Petals Unfurled

In a garden where giggles grow tall,
Butterflies stumble; they frolic and fall,
A flower named Belle wears a crown of fuzz,
While daisies gossip, full of good buzz.

Pansies prance, all colors set free,
Roses puff out, singing, 'Look at me!'
Sunflowers chuckle, waving with glee,
In this lovely chaos, what a sight to see!

Each petal's a jester, spinning around,
With roots in the earth, they make joyful sounds,
Blossoms bloom wide, with a wink and a whirl,
In this silly garden, watch the laughter unfurl.

So join the parade of petals and cheer,
Where joy is the soil, cultivate the sincere,
With every soft giggle and snicker, we yield,
In this tender land, let love be revealed!

The Color of Affection

In a garden of socks, I found your shoe,
With a smell like old cheese, but I still love you.
You paint with ketchup, I bake with jam,
Together we mix in a fabulous slam!

Your hair's like a squirrel, all wild and bright,
I laugh when you dance, your moves give me fright.
Like two peas in a pod, we tangle and wrap,
You pick my nose, I say, 'Let's take a nap!'

With crayons and laughter, we color the day,
Your giggles like music, they brighten my way.
We'll skip through the puddles, we'll hop like a frog,
In this silly love, you're my favorite smog.

So here's to the chaos, the playful and strange,
In the mess of affection, we'll never exchange.
Like mismatched socks, we're just meant to be,
Oh, doodle-poo darling, come waltz next to me!

A Harvest of Memories

In a field of bananas, we danced with glee,
You slipped and fell, what a sight to see!
We gathered up laughter, like pumpkins in fall,
Each chuckle we shared, a bright orange ball.

With socks on our heads, we spun like a top,
You made me a crown from a lollipop!
We picnicked on pizza, we drank apple juice,
In our silly kingdom, there's no such excuse.

We planted old jokes like seeds in the ground,
In the garden of laughter, our humor abounds.
With a wink and a smile, we water each pun,
Our harvest of giggles is never done.

So here's to our orchard, the weird and the wild,
In the realms of the funny, we're forever a child.
Side by side we'll frolic, through fields of delight,
In this quirky adventure, everything's bright!

Nature's Romance

The bees and the flowers wear silly hats,
As we run through the meadows, just two silly rats.
You tripped over daisies, then laughed like a loon,
When the frogs joined the dance, we howled at the moon.

Underneath the great oak, we made our own rules,
We grilled up some jokes, like two backyard fools.
With squirrels as our audience, we put on a show,
I dropped my punchline, it fell like a toe!

The clouds were our pillows, the sun our big friend,
In this wacky adventure, there's no need to pretend.
With leaves like confetti, we danced in the breeze,
Nature's a joker, and we laugh with ease.

Just two peas in the pod, let the giggles ignite,
With humor as our compass, we'll soar through the night.

So here's to the silly, the light and the sweet,
In this funny romance, our hearts skip a beat!

Sweet Whispers of Desire

In the garden of giggles we play,
Where we tripped over hearts in a silly ballet.
Bumblebees buzz with a cheeky grin,
As we daintily dance, letting the fun begin.

Your winks are the fruit of a mischievous tree,
And every laugh bounces, oh so carefree.
With marshmallow clouds overhead we float,
While our jokes sail high like a buoyant boat.

Tickle me tender, let's share a slice,
Of cake and sweet chaos, oh so nice.
With frosting and sprinkles, we conquer the day,
In this funny romance, let's frolic and play!

The Bounty of Togetherness

Two peas in a pod, we giggle and squint,
Like pickles on pizza, it's weird but we hint.
In the orchard of quirks, we harvest delight,
Our laughter's a fruit that's juicy and bright.

Bouncing like grapes, we roll down the hill,
While squirrels throw acorns, oh what a thrill!
We toast with the sun, sipping lemonade,
And dance like two chickens, in a joyful parade.

With inside jokes ripening, oh what a fun,
Our bond is a harvest that's just begun.
From puns to pranks, we're a colorful crew,
In the orchard of laughter, just me and you!

Juicy Embrace

In a field of giggles, we frolic and squeeze,
Like oranges oozing, we're never at ease.
Your laugh is a nectar, sweet as can be,
An embrace full of sunshine, come squeeze next to me.

With candy-corn kisses and jellybean dreams,
Together we're silly, bursting at the seams.
Like fruit in a salad, so random and bright,
Who knew we'd end up a hilarious sight?

Let's dance in the rain with our candy umbrella,
And sing off-key to our favorite fella.
In this juicy adventure, we're never alone,
With giggles for currency, we've found a home!

Blossom and Bloom

Like daisies and dandelions, we sway in the breeze,
With puns that are sprouting, putting hearts at ease.
We twirl in the meadow, with petals galore,
Our laughter a fragrance that's hard to ignore.

With sunshiney smiles, we play peek-a-boo,
Twirling like tulips, with each silly view.
Your jokes are the nectar that fuels every laugh,
While we chase after butterflies, sharing a gaffe.

As seasons unfold in a colorful spree,
Our blooming connection is destined to be.
With hearts intertwining, just look at us zoom,
Like flowers in spring, we're in perfect bloom!

Sweet Lullabies of the Heart

In the garden of giggles, we dance and we sway,
Picking fruits of our laughter, come what may.
A banana slips past, it's a slippery thrill,
I'll catch you my dear, if you're ready—chill!

The apples are chatting, oh what a surprise,
Discussing our future beneath sunny skies.
With lemons so zesty, they're making a scene,
Our fruit salad love, it's a citrusy dream!

Pineapples smiling, with crowns on their heads,
We share all our secrets as darkness spreads.
In this sweet chaos, our hearts start to sing,
Together we tumble, oh what joy we bring!

So let's climb the trees, let's swing from the line,
In this orchard of joy, your heart's nestled mine.
Though the fruits might be messy, I'll cherish each part,
For it's the funny moments that pull at the heart.

Tender Vines

Through tangled up laughter, we twist and we twine,
Like grapes hanging low, we sip sweet red wine.
You made a bad pun, I snorted with glee,
Our joy woven tightly, just you and me.

The cucumbers giggle, they can't quite compete,
With our starlit debates on which snack is sweet.
In this patch of delight, the pumpkins all cheer,
Let's dance on the vines, with no hints of fear!

Tomatoes are blushing as I steal a kiss,
While the peppers look on, "What's all this bliss?"
In the rows of our garden, the love's really neat,
We tell silly jokes while we plant tiny feet.

These vines of our banter grow stronger each day,
In a patch of delight, we frolic and play.
With veggies around us, we cultivate cheer,
Our tenderest moments are perfectly clear!

Ripening Emotions

In a world full of fruit flies, we plot and conspire,
Your smile's like jam, it ignites my desire.
Mangoes are winking, they know what's in store,
A kitchen dance party? Oh, let's have some more!

With cherries a-chatter, and peaches so sweet,
We're mixing emotions, oh what a treat!
The fruits conspire softly, creating a buzz,
Our hearts like a blender, are whirling because…

You slip on a peel, and we both fall in haste,
Laughter erupts as we share frosty paste.
The bananas take bets on what's next for us two,
We're ripening nicely, just like fruit stew.

So let's savor the moments, as silly as they are,
With fruit bowl confessions, we'll raise the bizarre.
In this blend of emotions, we squish and we blend,
It's a fruity adventure, with you I'll transcend!

Golden Hours Together

When the sun hits the horizon, it's time for some fun,
Like popped popcorn kernels, we've only begun.
The cozy warmth fills the air with delight,
As shadows chase giggles, while we hold on tight.

With buttered-up stories that drench us in glee,
We're floating like marshmallows in sweet jubilee.
Gold in the sky, yet our hearts are aglow,
Come join in the laughter, let's put on a show!

A picnic on blankets with sandwiches stacked,
Strawberries whispering, "Hey, let's hit the snack!"
Chasing fireflies, we dance way past the hour,
In these golden moments, you're my favorite flower.

As day turns to dusk, we'll snuggle and sigh,
In this blanket of laughter, just you and I.
With fun on the menu and love on the plate,
These golden hours shared, oh, they're just first-rate!

Abundant Yearnings

In a garden, I wait for fate,
Peaches giggle, too ripe to debate.
Tomatoes flirt, their skins all red,
But none offer me a slice of bread.

Cucumbers whisper, 'Come take a bite!'
Carrots chuckle, 'We're quite the sight!'
I ponder love in fragrant blooms,
While squirrels dance in nature's rooms.

A beet says, 'Hey, you look so sweet!'
But I just trip over my own feet.
In this jungle of veggies, I sigh,
Maybe I'll find romance in a pie.

So here I stand in my veggie patch,
Dreaming of someone to make me hatch.
With a heart all tangled, absurd and true,
I'll find my soulmate—maybe in stew!

Savoring Each Moment

Banana peels slip with a giggle,
As I wiggle and dance, just a little.
Ice cream drips down my eager cone,
With every lick, I feel less alone.

Cherries bounce in a bowl of cheer,
While jellybeans whisper, 'Come near!'
Grapes gossip about their big crush,
As I munch on popcorn, feeling the rush.

Pineapples say, 'We're the life of the party!'
While I juggle fruit, acting quite naughty.
Mangoes wink, oh what a scene,
In this fruity circus, I'm the queen!

So I'll savor each laugh, small and sweet,
As flavors collide, oh what a treat!
In this carnival of joy and delight,
Every moment's a romp and a bite!

The Taste of Connection

Pickles and mustard, a savory pair,
Whisper sweet secrets like they truly care.
LOve's like a burger, juicy and grand,
With fries on the side, a golden strand.

Chocolate and peanut butter unite,
Creating a dream that feels just right.
Pasta twirls with a flirty swirl,
As meatballs giggle, oh what a whirl!

Veggies all gather for a dance,
But broccoli's shy, it won't take a chance.
Avocado smiles and gives a nod,
"Together, we'll create something odd!"

Tuna and crackers, what a delight,
Crafting connections, oh what a sight!
In the banquet of life, let's take a leap,
Savoring laughter, memories to keep!

Nature's Caress

The sun peeks out with a wink and grin,
As flowers bloom, let the fun begin.
Butterflies flutter, all dressed in hues,
While bees hum tunes, spreading the news.

A squirrel swings by, wearing a hat,
Says, "Life's too short, let's have a chat!"
Leaves rustle softly, sharing their tales,
While the wind laughs at the bouncing trails.

Clouds roll by, doing silly tricks,
As the sun plays tag, oh what a mix!
In gardens of whims, where joy takes flight,
Air filled with giggles, everything's right.

With nature around, let's dance 'til dark,
Embracing the laughter, igniting the spark.
In this enchanted realm, I find peace,
In the rhythm of nature, my worries cease!

Symphony of Blossoms

In a garden where giggles bloom,
Butterflies twist like they're in a cartoon.
Daisies chatter with a sunny flair,
While bees dance like they haven't a care.

Tulips gossip in colors bright,
About the roses that flirt all night.
With petals fluttering, oh what a show,
Their jokes in the breeze, just steal the flow.

Sunflowers stand tall, they're quite the sight,
Swaying to music that feels just right.
They wink at the daisies, share a quick grin,
While the garden throws a party to win.

In this symphony, laughter's the key,
Every bloom joins in, it's a jubilee.
Nature's concert, a silly ballet,
Where petals play tag, and love's here to stay.

Petal-Soft Dreams

In a field of dreams where petals play,
A daisy tried flirting, in its own way.
With a breeze so gentle, it whispered a tune,
"Oh tulip, I think my heart's gone maroon!"

The lilacs burst out; they couldn't refrain,
"Love is a dance that drives us insane!"
Tulips responded, "Oh what a delight,
With petals so soft, let's party all night!"

Bees joined the fun in a jazzy attire,
While butterflies twirled, lifted higher and higher.
With laughter and giggles, they filled up the air,
Making flower dreams float, without a care.

So let's toast to blooms, to laughter and cheer,
In this petal-soft world, we'll hold love dear.
For whimsy and wonder, we can't get enough,
In this garden of joy, we'll share all our stuff.

Vibrant Connections

In a patch of wildflowers, oh what a sight,
Sunshine made the petals twirl in delight.
A clover asked, "Hey, wanna dance with me?"
While a buttercup giggled, "Yes, let it be!"

Dandelions chuckled, their seeds taking flight,
As they spun through the air like kites in the night.
"Catch me if you can!" the wildflowers said,
In a game of love, with hearts full of red.

The daisies formed circles, their laughter a blast,
Creating connections that made moments last.
Every color was buzzing, it was plain to see,
That in this explosion, there's magic to be!

So here's to bright blooms and connections alive,
Where laughter is fragrant, and friendships thrive.
In a world painted vibrant, with joy all around,
These moments and memories forever abound.

Cherished Groves

Under the trees, where the apples grow,
Fruits crack jokes, with a sweetened glow.
"Hey peach, you're fuzzy, but we think you're neat,
With laughter so juicy, can't be beat!"

In groves where the orange slices start to sway,
Fruit friends gather, for a lively display.
"Let's form a band, with rhythm and cheer,
Jamming together as the harvest draws near!"

Cherries giggled, gave their best wink,
While pears made a joke that made everyone rethink.
Laughter rang out, from a lemon so bold,
"Sharing's the secret, let the stories unfold!"

So here in the cherished, the laughter won't cease,
In this grove of delight, we'll dance with ease.
With fruits all united in a colorful play,
These moments together brighten the day!

Nectar of Togetherness

In a garden where laughter grows,
Two bees buzz and dance, as everyone knows.
They sip on sweet nectar, oh what a treat,
Dancing on flowers with wobbly feet.

Sunshine smiles, painting petals bright,
The bees make a plan for a flight at night.
They share silly secrets, as they take a chance,
In the hive of their hearts, they spin and prance.

A flower says, "Honey, why don't we sing?"
The bees hum along—it's a joyous fling.
With pollen in pockets, they twirl and sway,
Creating sweet memories at the end of the day.

Together they bumble, through thick and thin,
Crafting their dreams, where the fun begins.
In this hive of giggles, they'll always stay,
As long as the flowers make them ballet!

Embrace Beneath the Canopy

Under trees that whisper secrets loud,
Two squirrels chuckle, feeling quite proud.
With acorns aplenty, they play hide and seek,
In their quirky dance, not a word to speak.

Nature's canopy spread like a show,
Tickling each pet with a gentle blow.
They leap and bound from branch to branch,
In a nutty adventure, they boldly prance.

With each silly twist, and cartwheel so grand,
They tumble and giggle, hand in hand.
Down comes a raindrop, oh what a splash!
They dance in puddles, making a splash!

Nestled in warmth of their leafy abode,
They share funny tales of their nutty road.
As twilight descends, their laughter takes flight,
Beneath their green galaxy, they embrace the night.

Chasing Sunsets Hand in Hand

Two clowns in sandals, why not run?
Chasing a sunset, oh what fun!
With bright red noses and floppy shoes,
They dance like no one, with nothing to lose.

The sky blazes pink, they wiggle their toes,
Painting each moment, all in good prose.
A tumble, a giggle, they trip on a log,
But laughter erupts, not a single fog.

They wave at the clouds, waving back in glee,
Playing tag with shadows, wild as can be.
With popcorn in hand, they hop on their feet,
"Every sunset is better when we share a treat!"

As the sun dips low, and day starts to sway,
They'll keep on chasing, come what may.
For in this delightful, whimsical race,
Joy's the prize that they always embrace.

The Allure of Juicy Promises

In a market of dreams, where giggles abide,
Two fruity characters, side by side.
An apple and orange, they share witty jokes,
With zesty puns to liven the folks.

"Hey there, my sweet, what's your zest?"
The orange replied, "I'm the very best!"
They roll and they tumble, in a citrus dance,
With a splash of laughter, they twirl and prance.

They whisper of plans, juicy and grand,
Creating fruit salads, oh isn't it bland?
With a sprinkle of sugar and a squeeze of lime,
They concoct a recipe sweeter than rhyme.

As the day wanes on, with each tasty bite,
They savor the giggles beneath the moonlight.
With every slice shared, their connection grows,
In the world of flavors, love's the way it flows.

The Language of Petals

In springtime blooms, a secret shared,
A flirt with bees, all unprepared.
Daisies giggle, tulips wink,
Whispers float like wine, we drink.

The roses blush, what can they hide?
A thistle's prick? Just love's wild ride!
Petals dance, with wind they sway,
In this garden, let's play all day.

With scents that swirl, oh so enticing,
Even cacti join, quite surprising!
A moonlit chat, Dr. Dandelion,
Concocts romance, it's pure, no lyin'.

So steal a kiss from the wilting leaves,
And waltz with clovers, my heart believes.
In silence shared, beneath the trees,
Florets laugh softly, as love's a breeze.

Harvest Moon Serenade

Under the moon, we gather round,
With apples bright, love's laughter found.
Corn stalks sway, like giggling friends,
As pumpkin guts write love letters, pens!

The cider flows, it tickles the tongue,
While crickets chirp a song so young.
We dance with squash, they're quite the sight,
In this harvest, hearts take flight.

Beneath the stars, mischief takes form,
We toss acorns; endearment's warm.
An owl hoots, "What's all the fuss?"
We answer back, "We're here for us!"

Then gather round, do share your tale,
With tipsy gourd, and loves that sail.
In moonlight's grip, we twirl and spin,
Love's harvest, oh, let the fun begin!

Soft Hues of Desire

In pastel shades, love's canvas laid,
With cotton candy dreams displayed.
A tinge of peach and lemon zest,
In softest blends, we laugh the best.

With each petal's twirl, giggles arise,
Like rainbow sprinkles in sunny skies.
The hues of plush, they gleam and shine,
A palette fresh, oh, love's divine!

A splash of mint? Now that's unique!
Our colors clash, but hearts still speak.
In watercolor hues, we swim and play,
Creating art in a vibrant way.

So, dip your brush, let laughter flow,
In shades of joy, let romance grow.
With playful strokes, we make our mark,
In this fine art, love's a spark!

A Garden's Plea

Oh please, dear sun, don't shine too bright,
   We're planting seeds of pure delight.
    With every sprout, a giggle grows,
  In this garden plot, our affection shows.

    The daisies cry, "We want a date!"
   While sleepy violets just can't wait.
    To join the fun in this floral bash,
  As bees join in our sweet, mad dash.

    Snails slide in, dressed for the ball,
  While ladybugs share tales with all.
 The tulips tease, in the soft wind's tune,
    A secret dance beneath the moon.

   So heed this call, oh hearts so bold,
 In gardens where wild stories unfold.
 Let blossoms blush with laughter's jest,
As nature's chorus sings, we are blessed!

Harvesting Hearts

In the orchard of giggles, we play,
Picking fruits of laughter, day by day.
You throw me a wink from the apple tree,
I catch it with glee, oh, can't you see?

Basket full of blushes, I'm feeling bold,
Your silly jokes are worth their weight in gold.
We dance through the branches as leaves give chase,
With each wobble and wobble, we quicken our pace.

Neighbors all wonder what's taking so long,
They think we're just crazy, but we're just strong.
With heart-shaped pails, we fill them with mirth,
Gathering joy in a patch of pure worth.

So let's toast with cider, this harvest of cheer,
With you by my side, there's nothing to fear.
We'll tickle the stars as the night takes its hold,
In this orchard of laughter, love's story unfolds.

The Blooming Embrace

In a field of daffodils, you call my name,
We twirl in the sunshine, it's never the same.
You trip on your shoelace, and down you go,
I laugh so hard, it's a blooming show!

We pick daisies wearing crowns, what a sight,
Each flower a secret, a giggle, a bite.
The bees buzz around like they're part of the show,
But hey! Watch out, here comes a rogue crow!

Your cheeky grin blossoms as petals tease,
You whisper of dreams carried on the breeze.
With hugs that smell sweet, we dance 'neath the sun,
In this zany embrace, we've already won!

So let's plant our laughter beneath starlit skies,
With each silly moment, our spirits will rise.
We'll bloom into laughter, no worries, no fears,
In this garden of giggles, let's grow more years!

Fruits of Affection

Swapping bananas for smirks, we're quite the pair,
You juggle your apples, a romantic affair.
With a splash of mischief, you steal my peach,
A fruity allegiance, right out of reach!

Our picnic of giggles on a checkered spread,
Tastes better with you, that's what I said.
Watermelons rolling, oh what a sight,
As you crack a joke, I burst with delight!

Strawberries whisper sweet, a juicy song,
You squeeze lemon juice, but I don't mind strong.
We toast with our smoothies, a zany delight,
With each drop of laughter, we're high on life tonight!

So here's to our harvest, a playful affair,
In the orchard of whimsy, we frolic with flair.
Our board of fruit flavors, each one a treasure,
With you in my basket, there's no greater pleasure!

Sunkissed Whispers

In the glow of the sun, your humor shines bright,
With quirky remarks that take wing in flight.
We play hopscotch on clouds, feeling so free,
Bouncing off rainbows, just you and me!

You tease me with tales of our future grand,
Two sunflowers swaying, a comical band.
With petals a-swaying, we giggle and grin,
As the pollen of joy makes our heads spin!

The sun tickles noses while we roll on the ground,
Each laugh a flower that blooms all around.
Our whispers like breezes, so warm and so sweet,
In this garden of humor, we'll never know defeat!

So let's gather the moments, with sunshine and cheer,
Creating our memories, so vivid and clear.
In this world of whimsy, you're my best friend,
With a wink and a smile, our laughter won't end!

The Orchard of Us

In the orchard where we play,
Apples joke and pears delay.
Bumblebees buzz with glee,
While we sip sweet lemonade, carefree.

Bananas giggle in the sun,
Saying, "Peel us – it's all in fun!"
Lemons rolling down the lane,
Tickling toes, oh what a gain!

Cherries dance upon the breeze,
Making all the trees do tease.
With every laugh and every cheer,
Our fruity world becomes so clear!

So let's frolic in this place,
With sticky fingers, twinkling grace.
In this harvest, so divine,
We'll share our fruit, your heart is mine!

Warmth in Every Bite

Bite into that pastry treat,
Cinnamon swirls that can't be beat!
Chocolate chunks that make us smile,
A gooey hug for a while.

Cupcakes lined in colors bright,
Dance around, what a delight!
Sprinkles laughing on top so high,
Let's dive in, oh me, oh my!

Lemon tarts with a zesty twist,
A tasty chance that can't be missed.
Sugar cookies in a row,
Making mischief as we go!

In this kitchen, laughter's found,
With every nibble, joy's unbound.
Whisking memories, one big bite,
In our hearts, it feels just right!

The Perfumed Essence

In gardens where the daisies giggle,
Fragrant blooms do dance and wiggle.
Roses whisper sweet nothings near,
While butterflies swoon, that's quite clear!

Lavender's lull brings dreams afloat,
In a floral boat, let's rock and gloat.
Sunflowers stretch to catch a glance,
Join the pollen's wild romance!

Dandelions play hide and seek,
In the breeze, they softly peek.
Petals falling like confetti,
Make our hearts a little sweaty!

Scent of jasmine fills the air,
With giggles shared everywhere.
Let's twirl beneath the moonlit dome,
In this garden, we find our home!

Glistening Emotions

Dewdrops twinkle like our smiles,
Every moment, joy compiles.
In puddles, we splash with delight,
Chasing giggles into the night.

Stars above wink as they play,
While laughter dances, come what may.
Tickled toes in the cool, wet grass,
This fleeting joy, please let it last!

Rainy days bring silly fun,
Making memories out of sun.
Splashing colors everywhere,
Life's a canvas, so don't despair!

Glistening shines through every tear,
A touch of whimsy, a friendly cheer.
In this mess, together we glow,
With silly dreams, let's steal the show!

Garden of Longing

In the garden, weeds start to dance,
Bugs with bow ties take a chance.
Sunflowers giggle, they lean in tight,
While roses blush under moon's soft light.

Bees are buzzing with silly rhymes,
While daisies act as judges in mime.
Naps in the grass, oh what a thrill,
Love is sprouting, against all will!

Cucumbers wink, squashes munch,
Tomatoes chuckle, ready for lunch.
With every seed that we dare to sow,
The weeds turn sweet, in love's warm glow!

Harvest's upon us, it's all quite mad,
Dancing with veggies, who knew they had?
Laughter echoes through the blooming glade,
In this garden where flirty fun is made.

Lush Passions

In a jungle where bananas swing,
Coconuts dance on a leafy ring.
Mangoes blush, they've got a flair,
Papayas giggle, floating in the air.

Vines twirl round like a wicked tease,
Lianas laugh in the warm, sweet breeze.
Passionfruit whispers with cheeky charm,
While little frogs croak with a wink and a harm.

Cherries jive, colliding in zest,
Tangoing closely, they befriend the rest.
Let's smother the salad in laughter and cheer,
In this lush playground, love is the gear.

So grab your forks, and hold on tight,
For dinner's a riot, it feels so right.
In the heart of the greens, let mischief bloom,
For love is a salad, tossed with a boom!

Picking Dreams

In the orchard where dreams take flight,
Apples grin in the soft daylight.
Pears in rows, with a giggle and sway,
As we pick the fruit for a cheeky bouquet.

Spiders cheer on their webby threads,
While owls debate on the paths that we tread.
With every bite of that juicy treat,
Life becomes silly, oh what a feat!

Nothing like nectarines, sweet with delight,
Pumping up fun with each tasty bite.
In his and her baskets, oh what a sight,
Picking for joy, heartbeats ignite.

So let's blend our dreams in a crazy churn,
With zest and laughter, it's our turn.
In this orchard where mischief teems,
We gather our joy, we gather our dreams!

The Season of Us

When the calendar flips to fun and cheer,
Winks from the sun, the time is near.
Crickets pluck strings with a jolly sound,
As laughter bubbles right off the ground.

Pies cooling down on the window ledge,
Ticklish whispers from the garden hedge.
With hats so big, we're all set to play,
In the season where silliness holds sway.

Chasing shadows as the sun dips low,
With ice-cream cones that steal the show.
Sprinklers spraying like a love-struck fling,
In this flirty weather, we let our hearts sing.

So raise a toast with the friends we trust,
To the giggles and chaos, in laughter we thrust!
For in this silly season, we find our way,
Wrapped in joy, we'll forever stay!

The Whispering Grove

In the grove where giggles grow,
Squirrels dance, putting on a show.
Trees gossip in the afternoon light,
Bumbling bees sharing laughs in flight.

A frog croaks jokes from a leafy throne,
While shy mice laugh, not wanting to be known.
Leaves rustle with whispers of cheer,
As flowers nod, saying, 'Stay right here!'

Breezes tease the flowers' dresses,
As crickets offer their best guesses.
The sun dips low, a golden hue,
While nature's here to laugh with you.

Under canopies of leafy hues,
Love's found where the laughter brews.
In this grove where joy can thrive,
The heart can dance and feel alive!

Moonlit Rendezvous

Under moon's laugh, a funny sight,
Two shadows tango in the night.
A cat sneezes, the couple jumps,
Then trips over their own heart thumps.

Stars twinkle like winking eyes,
Swinging lanterns in the skies.
A giggling wind spins round and round,
As owls hoot, making silly sounds.

Love notes flutter like butterflies,
While party hats fall from the skies.
A ticklish breeze embraces tight,
As laughter echoes in the night.

Their hearts play tag, a chase so sweet,
As moonbeams dance on happy feet.
With each giggle, love finds a way,
In the air, come out to play!

Fruits of Passion

In a garden where the berries laugh,
Two hearts debate the perfect path.
Strawberries blushing with juicy glee,
While cherries debate, 'Who's the best me?'

Bananas crack jokes, slip on their peel,
Coconuts chuckle at their strong appeal.
Melons giggle, rolling away,
While lovers find their funky sway.

Grapes whisper secrets, a fruity choir,
As love simmers in a bubbling fryer.
A pie cools with a mischievous grin,
As laughter stews, let the fun begin!

Underneath a bough so sweet,
Where even the apples can't be beat.
In this orchard of joy and cheer,
Love's flavor blossoms far and near!

Lush Love Letters

In a field where daisies write,
Letters flutter in the light.
With petals whispering secrets bold,
Scribbles of warmth in red and gold.

A butterfly sends notes on the breeze,
While grasshoppers giggle, folding with ease.
The sun, a postman, smiles wide,
Delivers cheer with the warmth of the tide.

In the midst of thorns, a sweet bouquet,
Wraps playful words, come what may.
As ink flows fresh from a teasing quill,
The heart scribbles its joyous thrill.

With twinkling stars and laugh-filled skies,
Each note of love brings silly sighs.
In this lush, vibrant space we share,
Love's laughter lingers, floating in air!

www.ingramcontent.com/pod-product-compliance
Lightning Source LLC
Chambersburg PA
CBHW062111280426
43661CB00086B/452